OKLAHOMA

A Turner Educational Services, Inc. book. Based on the Portrait
of America television series created by R.E. (Ted) Turner.

Library of Congress Number: 86-17775

1234567890   9089888786

Library of Congress Cataloging in Publication Data

Thompson, Kathleen.
  Oklahoma.

  (Portrait of America)
  "A Turner book."
  Summary: Discusses the history, economy, culture,
and future of Oklahoma. Also includes a state
chronology, pertinent statistics, and maps.
  1. Oklahoma—Juvenile literature. I. Title.
II. Series: Thompson, Kathleen. Portrait of America.
F694.3.T48   1986   976.6   86-17775
ISBN 0-86514-456-7 (lib. bdg.)
ISBN 0-86514-531-8 (softcover)

Cover Photo: Oklahoma Tourism and Recreation Department

★ ★ ★ ★ ★

Portrait of AMERICA

OKLAHOMA

Kathleen Thompson

A TURNER BOOK
RAINTREE PUBLISHERS

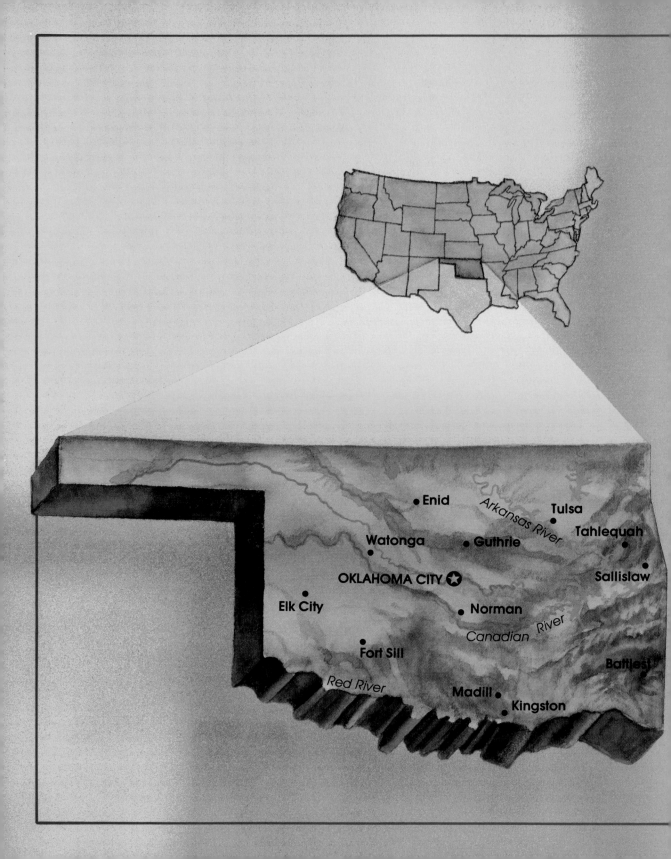

CONTENTS

Introduction

Oklahoma, the Sooner State.

"Oklahoma is a microcosm of the country and that's why it's been so hard for everyone to put Oklahoma in one part or the other."

Oklahoma: oil wells, cattle, cowboys, Indians, red clay.

"I think most Oklahomans . . . we're a cross between optimists and realists. We like to dream, but we also have to cut our dreams down to what we can meet."

So much happened so quickly in the making of Oklahoma! The result is a state where change is a part of life. There are booms and busts just as there are droughts and tornados and showers of oil pushing up and out of the earth.

And somehow Oklahomans seem to like it that way.

"Eighty-niner Day" at the Guthrie Rodeo.

The Red Land

Oklahoma has been, at one time or another, the land that no one wanted and the land that everyone wanted. Its history is wild, colorful, sometimes tragic. It's a story of booms and busts, cowboys and Indians, land rushes and gushers.

As a state, Oklahoma is less than a century old. But its history goes back to some of the earliest white explorations—and beyond.

Hundreds of years ago, Plains Indians hunted buffalo across Oklahoma's flatlands. They were the Kiowa, the Comanche, and the Kiowa-Apache. The Wichita and the Caddo farmed and built small towns.

In 1541, Francisco Vásquez de Coronado found Oklahoma

Wichita Mountains Wildlife Refuge.

A modern-day replica of a 17th-century Cherokee village at TSA-LA-GI Cherokee Heritage Center.

while searching for the Seven Cities of Cibola. The same year another great Spanish explorer, Hernando de Soto came, again looking for gold. They were the first, but not the last white men to make the mistake of thinking that Oklahoma held no riches in its red land. They turned around and went back. The Indians continued to farm and hunt buffalo.

But far away, their future was being decided by people they would never see. In 1682, France claimed Oklahoma as part of its Louisiana Territory. A little more than a hundred years later, in 1803, the United States bought the land as part of the Louisiana Purchase.

It was then that a new stage of Oklahoma history began. It was to be a time of sorrow beginning with one of the most shameful acts of the new United States government.

In the early 1800s, white settlers in the southeastern United States began to demand that all Indian lands in that area be opened for white settlement. That meant forcing the Indians to leave. These Indians belonged to five tribes—the Cherokee, Chickasaw, Choctaw, Creek, and Seminole.

These were people who had lived for hundreds of years in the same place. They had farms, stores, a newspaper. They had adopted many European customs and blended them with their own traditions. Suddenly, all they had was taken from them and they were forced to march, guarded by soldiers, through the wilderness to Oklahoma. Thousands of them died along the way. The path they took came to be known as the *Trail of Tears.*

A small part of these people managed to reach what was then called Indian Territory. With great courage, they began to rebuild their civilization.

Each of the tribes created a nation with written laws and a capital. They set up courts and law enforcement agencies. They built towns and schools. These five nations made treaties with the United States government that should have protected them.

"Trail of Tears," painted by Elizabeth Janes, depicts Indians of the southeast being forced off their land and into Oklahoma in the early 1800s.

They were guaranteed their land "as long as grass shall grow and rivers run."

They also built plantations and brought in black slaves to work on them.

And then came the Civil War. Because they were slaveholders, many of the people of the Indian Territory sided with the Confederacy. One Cherokee, Stand Watie, became a Confederate general. Many other Indians fought with the Union. The area suffered losses during the war that were as awful as any place in the nation.

After the war, the Union punished the Confederacy and all who had supported it. In the South, that meant many unwise and sometimes unfair laws. In the Indian Territory, Reconstruction meant more than that.

After the war, large parts of the Indians' land were taken away from them, the land that was to be theirs forever. They

General Stand Watie, the only Indian brigadier general in the Confederate Army, is pictured against a background of the Ouachita National Forest.

By 1889, most of Oklahoma was occupied by Indians who had been removed from their ancestral lands. Shown is a historic photo of some of the earliest settlers of Oklahoma City.

were forced to let railroads come through the land they were allowed to keep.

The result of all this was that the tribes of the Indian Territory had to start again from the ground up. And their troubles were not over.

About ten years later, the cattle drives began. White men from surrounding areas herded their cattle to markets like Kansas City across Indian land, rifles ready to fight anyone who opposed them.

More Indians were brought into the Indian Territory from the north and the east. By 1889, most of Oklahoma was occupied by Indian tribes who had been forced out of their own ancestral lands. Here in the Indian Territory, they were told, they could stay. It was a sad compromise for these people, but at least they had some kind of home.

The compromise would not last. There was one area in the middle of the territory that had not yet been assigned to any tribe. White settlers began to come into the territory, headed for that land. At first, the U.S. Army turned them back. But then, in 1889, Congress opened the land to white settlement.

Above, prairie schooners make their way to the "Promised Land" of Oklahoma in 1889. At left, homesteaders stake their claims.

The land rushes into Oklahoma Territory are among the most colorful events in American history. On the morning of April 22, 1889, 50,000 white homesteaders lined up on the border of what had once been Creek and Seminole land. A pistol was shot and they poured in. By nightfall, claims were staked and two cities of 10,000 people were created.

A year later, Oklahoma Territory was officially a reality. It was an island of white settlement in the middle of the Indian Territory. But not for long. Demands continued to open more Indian land to whites.

In 1891, the U.S. government began dividing tribal lands. Allotments were made to individual members of each tribe. The rest of the land was opened to whites in a series of "runs."

In the eastern part of the territory, the tribes had some experience in farming. They were able to take their allotments and, in some cases, create prosperous farms.

In the western part of the territory were tribes whose entire culture depended on hunting and moving freely over large areas of tribal land. These people knew nothing about farming. They were easy prey for white settlers who bought their allotments, giving them enough to keep their families alive for a short time.

Although deprived of their land and taken advantage of, the people of the five tribes were still courageous and ready to work with their white neighbors. The leaders of the tribes called a convention in 1905. They invited white citizens of the Indian Territory to be part of the convention, which adopted a constitution for the state of Sequoyah. The constitution was approved, but Congress refused to accept the new state because it did not include Oklahoma Territory.

At that time in the Indian Territory white settlers outnumbered Indians five to one. Oklahoma Territory was entirely white. Congress insisted that the Twin Territories, as they were called, enter the Union together, as one state.

In 1907, they did. Oklahoma became the 46th state in the Union. Its capital was Guthrie.

But the drama and color of Oklahoma history did not end with statehood. In a way, it was just beginning. In the next few years, one governor "stole" the state seal from Guthrie to make Oklahoma City the state capital. Two other governors were impeached, one for calling out the National Guard to prevent a grand jury from meeting. It was

the twentieth century, but in Oklahoma, the West was still wild.

During this time, farmers were discovering that the homesteads they had been allowed by the government were just too small. They had been based on the size of a profitable farm in the East and Midwest, where the soil was much more fertile. Oklahoma land was good for grazing cattle, but no single homestead was big enough to

support a herd.

With low farm prices, farmers in Oklahoma were in trouble. But something else was happening to Oklahoma's economy. Oil and gas were discovered in Osage County and then in the Great Seminole Oil Field. Oil poured up out of the red clay soil.

In 1930 Governor William H. "Alfalfa Bill" Murray decided that too much oil was pouring up. Prices were dropping. So Murray simply shut down 3,000 oil wells. He kept them shut down for three months, waiting for oil prices to rise again.

And then came the Dust Bowl. It was the time of the Great Depression and the whole country was suffering terrible hardship. In Oklahoma and the states surrounding it, nature joined in to make things worse.

Rain stopped falling from the sky. The sun beat down and baked the dry land. High winds churned the soil into dust and blew it away. Dust storms blotted out the sun.

With no crops to feed their families, farmers loaded their belongings onto cars and pickup trucks and left Oklahoma to look for work.

World War II began to bring prosperity back to Oklahoma. Oil was badly needed and Oklahoma could provide it. New farming methods brought many Oklahoma farms back to life. Also, Oklahoma now had forty-one military bases.

On the left-hand page is an oil refinery (top) and a natural gas well (bottom). Above is an onshore oil well in Oklahoma's Anadarko Basin.

Don Sibley

In the years that followed, dams were built and lakes created to improve the water supply. With its abundant supplies of fuel, Oklahoma now became an ideal location for industry.

Reforms were made in education, finances, and the prison sys-

At left is the Salina Pumped Storage Project. The Pensacola Powerhouse generators are pictured below. Turner Falls near Davis on the right-hand page (top) provides relaxation and beauty for Oklahoma visitors. At the bottom is an air boat on Great Salt Plains Lake.

Don Sibley

tem. The new lakes and a growing state park system brought in tourists.

Oklahoma today still shows signs of its youth. It is not all that far from the days when the Plains Indians hunted buffalo, when the five Indian nations struggled to hold on to their civilizations. Oklahoma is not so grown up that it can't change in ways that are hard to predict.

That's part of the charm of Oklahoma.

Oklahoma Tourism and Recreation Department

U.S. Fish and Wildlife Service, Photo by John A. Kirk

A Tale of Two Tribes

"Cherokee National Industries was a company that started in 1969. Since that time the company has grown to a point where today we employ over 270 people. We have gross sales that will approach 10 million dollars next year."

That's not the kind of talk most people expect to hear from an Indian chief. But Ross Swimmer, former tribal chief of Oklahoma's Cherokee Nation, does not fit easily into stereotypes.

The Cherokees never have.

The Cherokees were one of the Five Civilized Tribes who were forced to march from the southeastern United States to Indian Territory in the early 1800s. They left behind them farms, towns, stores, newspaper offices. They had a written language, thriving businesses, and a highly developed culture.

"The Cherokee heritage, as well as that of the other Five Civilized Tribes—we had a lot of statesmen. We had people that were capable of dealing with Congress in those early times, the formative years of this country. And I think that is one of the main . . . differences that we have with the tribes in the West."

Of course, the Cherokee's ability to deal with the white man's culture did not protect them from the terrible hardships felt by Native Americans across the country. But it did give them an edge. And today the Cherokee people are finding ways to integrate with the dominant culture. Most of all, they are creating jobs.

Here is what Swimmer said when he was chief. *"It's part of my work as the Principal Chief of the tribe to make sure that companies like this and others that the Cherokee Nation owns are able to keep a good supply of work coming in. Our goal is employment."*

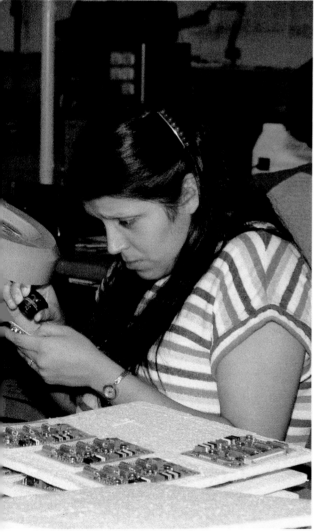

Photos by U.S. Department of the Interior

Assistant Secretary of the Interior for Indian Affairs Ross O. Swimmer is in the foreground. At left, a Cherokee woman works on components for the space program at Cherokee National Industries in Stillwater.

Ross Swimmer, Wilma Mankiller (the present chief), and the other 60,000 Cherokees in Oklahoma are reconciling progress and tradition. But in southwestern Oklahoma 200 Apaches are doing their best just to get by.

The Apaches were Plains Indians. They moved from place to place, hunting and living off the land. When the white men came, it was a conflict between two entirely different cultures. Neither side understood the other. The Apaches did not have statesmen to negotiate with Congress. They had proud warriors like Geronimo, who was finally promised that the tribe could remain on their land "as long as the sun rises, the grass grows, and the water runs." And then . . .

"Geronimo came home one day to find his whole family killed. And he made a vow that from that day on he would kill every white man and every Mexican that he saw. So for twenty-seven years they (the Apaches) were held prisoners of war. That's from 1886 until 1913. All those twenty-seven years they wanted to go back to their homeland and they were promised that they would be sent back. Those promises were always broken."

Mildred Cleghorn's painful words about the Apache people give only a small glimpse of the destruction of a culture.

"We have literally lost our language. . . . Our people wouldn't be here today if our great-grandfathers didn't decide to surrender. They gave up so much of their life so that we as younger people can be here today. And I think that all that I can do is just keep that alive."

Mildred Cleghorn, as tribal leader, works hard to keep the tribe together and the traditions alive. She would like someday to create a small industry to provide work for the Apaches. In the meantime, there is a tribal complex built in 1976 with a

Apache tribal leader Mildred Cleghorn, who is dedicating her life to keeping Apache culture alive, is on the left-hand page. Above is a 1913 photo of Apache women being deported from their ancestral homeland. Circled is Mildred Cleghorn's mother. Mildred's father, who was an Apache scout, is pictured in a historic photo at the right.

small day-care center that makes it easier for the tribe members to go out and find work. It's difficult, but . . .

". . . we didn't want to disappear from the face of the earth and just leave . . . leave nothing."

A Hard Place to Leave

"I just began a teaching career, and we heard there was a job here teaching. It took us all day to find Battiest, and when we did find it, my wife and I talked it over. And we said, since jobs were kind of scarce, we would take this job. But it would strictly be for a year or two. Here it is thirty years later and I'm still here."

The small town of Battiest in southeastern Oklahoma seems to be a hard town to leave. School-teacher Tom Lowry hasn't managed in thirty years. Jim Harris, who runs the country store, tried to leave Battiest after college.

"I had a very good job. I worked in marketing with a farm equipment company and then my last position was regional manager for the entire western United States. And I probably made three times what I'm making here. But we were very unhappy."

So what is it that keeps people in Battiest? As you might have guessed, it isn't money.

"Our economy is very stable here. It's usually rotten."

Jim Harris runs the country store in Battiest.

Paxson D. Smith

24

It isn't an easy life, not according to Charlotte Parsons.

"*We raise a few cows, have the chicken houses, try to raise our own food. We just have to do several things and work hard at all of them to make a living.*"

But there is something here. There is a love for the hilly land, so different from most of Oklahoma. There is a slower pace to life. And, according to Kim Parsons, there are values.

"*My parents, in my childhood, they gave me everything a child could ever need—not always every material thing, but the things that were important. . . . We always felt secure. Our family felt secure. And they were always exactly the example of what they wanted us children to be. My mother and dad both work real hard and they work long hours. And they taught us how to work. And they taught us how to be happy with the simple things. . . . It's so peaceful here. I don't know why anybody would ever want to leave.*"

Peace, simple things, hard work, close families. Those are the things that make Battiest a hard place to leave. Kim's father,

Paxson D. Smith

At the right is a chicken house on the Parson's farm. On the right-hand page are (top) Andy Parsons and (bottom) Charlotte Parsons.

Billy Parsons, puts it very clearly.
"I could sure use a million dollars, but if it meant that I had to leave this country and never return, then I'd turn it down."

Gushers and Government

Oklahoma has an oil well on the grounds of the state capitol building. That might give you an idea of how important oil is to this southwestern state.

There is oil almost everywhere in Oklahoma. Cattle ranchers have oil wells in the middle of their grazing land. Farmers have oil wells in the back forty. Mining—particularly oil production—is the single largest area of economic activity in Oklahoma.

That doesn't mean that everyone in the state has an oil well in the backyard or even that most people get up in the morning and go to work in the oil fields. In fact, there are almost as many people employed in agriculture as in mining. But mining brings about $10 billion a year into Oklahoma's

The state capitol building in Oklahoma City.

economy, more than three times what is brought in by agriculture.

Where there is oil, there is often natural gas, Oklahoma's second most important mining product. Natural gas liquids

The sterile manufacture of electronic computer equipment (left) is a growing Oklahoma industry. The state's most important crop, winter wheat, is harvested below.

such as butane are third. Stone and helium gas are the other significant mining industries.

Oklahoma's manufacturing brings in more than $8 billion a year. Nonelectrical machinery is the largest area of manufacture. Much of this industry is directly connected to the oil fields. Oil field machinery and equipment are manufactured in many parts of the state. And the manufacturing of electronic computer equipment is a growing industry.

Another important area of manufacturing is fabricated metal products. The goods made from metal in Oklahoma factories include metal barrels, cans, and drums, many of which are used in the oil industry. They also include hand tools and heating equipment.

Oklahoma's factories make rubber and plastic products, petroleum and coal products, transportation equipment, and many other varied products. This part of Oklahoma's economy grows every year.

Agriculture is still vital to life in Oklahoma. Cattle are as common a sight as oil wells. They're Oklahoma's top-ranked source of agricultural income. But they are not the state's only important farm product.

The most important field crop is winter wheat. Hay is second and other important crops include corn, cotton, peanuts, soybeans, and sorghum grain. Greenhouse and nursery products rank high as well. And if you've ever eaten an Oklahoma pecan pie, you know that there are things besides cash income that can make a crop important.

One of the interesting things about the Oklahoma economy is that the second largest single group of workers is government employees. More people work for the federal, state, and local governments than are employed in mining and manufacturing combined. They work at one of the many military installations or at the Federal Aviation Administration.

All in all, the economy of Oklahoma is strong and varied. And there are still opportunities for new and different enterprises.

Living Legend

"It's time now for Virgie White, your live-wire reporter speaking to us from beautiful Lake Texoma Lodge. Now, heeere's Virgie!"

What do you have to do to become a legend in your own time? Start a successful rock group? Win three Academy Awards? Make a billion dollars? Virgie White did it by caring about people.

Born in Indian Territory before Oklahoma became a state, Virgie has worked as a waitress since 1916. At eighty-eight, she's still going strong—working at Lake Texoma Lodge, calling in to Madill Radio Station KMAD on her work break to tell about interesting people and good causes, writing a weekly column for the newspaper, visiting the senior citizen center, speaking at fund-raising events for the youth club. It makes a person tired just to think about it. It doesn't seem to faze Virgie.

Virgie White is shown on the right-hand page receiving an award from the Oklahoma Hotel and Motel Association. At age 88, she still works as a waitress at a lodge on picturesque Lake Texoma at right.

"I was never tired a day in my life. When we worked in the fields, we'd go to work before daylight. We'd milk cows, feed hogs, you know, and when everybody else was dead tired and about ready to drop dead, I was out jumping a rope, throwing a ball over the house. I don't know. I just never was tired in my life."

Virgie White's unfailing energy and optimism have made her a force for good in her community. Her interest and intelligence have made her someone to pay attention to. Carl Albert listens to Virgie and has since before he became Speaker of the House of

Oklahoma Tourism and Recreation Department

Representatives.

"First time I ever met her was the first time I was running for Congress. I pulled in a little late out to the edge of Madill to stop at a little restaurant there, met her. She went out with me. We sat in my car and talked for about three hours. She gave me the only real lesson I ever had on Marshall County. Didn't need another one once you talked to Virgie."

Virgie White can look back on a happy, useful life as a loved and respected member of her community. But Virgie doesn't look back. She always looks forward.

"Well, I'm an optimist. I feel like that somewhere around the corner I'm going to be able to do something better than I've ever done before."

Now that's what legends are made of.

Cowboys and Indians

"**I** never met a man I didn't like."

Famous words. Familiar words. People who don't know anything else about Will Rogers—one of Oklahoma's contributions to the world—know those words. They say a lot about Will Rogers and almost as much about the state he called his home.

People in Oklahoma smile. They shake your hand. You can convince them not to like you, but you have to work at it. There's an openness about this state that probably comes out of its history. The people who came here in the beginning were all starting fresh. They just about had to take each other at face value.

That same openness can be seen in the culture of the state.

Will Rogers never met a man he didn't like.

Woody Guthrie Publication

Oklahoma legend Woody Guthrie is pictured in a 1935 photo with "Lefty Lou" Crisswell. The two performed frequently on their radio show in Los Angeles.

cowboy there stands the model for the monumental tribute to Oklahoma's Indians—*The End of the Trail.*

It's important to remember that this is a place where the first newspapers were the *Cherokee Advocate* and the *Choctaw Indian*

A good example is the Cowboy Hall of Fame in Oklahoma City. Here, the people who worked hard on the open range are honored right next to movie cowboys like John Wayne and Gene Autry. The paintings and sculptures of great western artists Charles Russell and Frederick Remington fill one room; spurs and saddles fill another. Beside all these tributes to the

Oklahoma City Convention and Tourism Bureau

Champion, written and published before white settlers ever came to the territory. Oklahoma is not only the home of the Cowboy Hall of Fame, but also is the home of the National Hall of Fame for American Indians at Anadarko.

Also throughout the state there are community theater groups, dozens of art and history museums, and musical groups. Oklahoma's two largest cities provide a variety of cultural opportunities. But don't ask the people in Oklahoma City to tell you about Tulsa or vice versa.

The Mummer Players perform "Li'l Abner" at left. Below is "The Admirable Outlaw" by N.C. Wyeth. The painting hangs in the Cowboy Hall of Fame.

Cowboy Hall of Fame

A Tale of Two Cities

"*Less than one hundred years ago the area that we see around us was an open grasslands mixed with river bottom. The people that lived in Tulsa at that time were Cherokees, Creeks, Choctaws, Chickasaws, Delawares. . . . Then the land rush happened.*"

The land rush happened. The oil rush happened. Business and industry came. And Tulsa grew up in the middle of the grassland.

Tulsa is not the capital of Oklahoma. It is not the state's largest city. But Tulsa is very proud of itself. In Tulsa you will find a symphony, an opera company, two very fine museums—the Gilcrease and the Phillbrook—and a commitment on the part of its businesses to cultivate Tulsa's image as a city of culture. Ed Wade, curator of the Phillbrook's collection of western art, puts it this way.

"*The men and women who made Tulsa, such as the Phillips who created Phillbrook and also part of the cultural history of what this city is, were adventurers. They took chances. Sometimes they won; sometimes they lost. Maybe that's called entrepreneurialism. But whatever it is, it showed something about a new area that allowed people a chance to take their talents, put it against the land, find what was possible and, just like Phillbrook, rather than copy what was acceptable on the East or acceptable on the West, they looked to the world.*"

Don Sibley

Dr. Edwin L. Wade is pictured with the Phillbrook Art Center where he is curator of art. The art center is the former home of Oklahoma oilman Waite Phillips.

Phillbrook Art Center

The people of Oklahoma City would argue about what part of the country influences Tulsa lifestyle.

"Tulsa looks east."

Those are the words of Oklahoma City businessman Robert Hefner. There's a real rivalry in Oklahoma between its two largest cities. Both cities have varied economies, but in the state known for oil and cattle, Tulsa seems to have more oil and Oklahoma City more cattle.

"The Oklahoma National Stockyards Company started operation in 1910. Today, it's the largest cattlemarket in the nation, handling in excess of one million head of cattle each year and about a quarter of a million head of hogs."

Along with the stockyards, Oklahoma City boasts the Cowboy Hall of Fame and a large, modern arts complex which includes the Oklahoma Theater Center and one of the best summer musical theater companies in the western United States. On the other hand, a lot of people in Tulsa wear cowboy hats.

Oklahoma City businessman Robert Hefner is pictured against a photo of the city's National Stockyards Company, the largest cattlemarket in the nation.

Oklahoma City Convention and Tourism Bureau

41

Oklahoma Tomorrow

"*Well, I'm an optimist. I feel like that somewhere around the corner I'm going to be able to do something better than I've ever done before.*"

The words are Virgie White's. But they express a feeling you find all over Oklahoma. Maybe it's the newness of the state. Maybe it's the wildcat spirit of the people who came here to claim land or dig oil wells. To the people who came here from all over the country, Oklahoma represented possibilities. It still does.

In the last several decades, Oklahoma's economy has been growing. Its public services such as schools have been getting better and better. The optimism of Oklahomans makes sense.

At the same time, there are problems. There are still

Tulsa, the "Oil Capital of the World," is Oklahoma's second largest city.

pockets of poverty and unemployment, many of them in Indian communities. The question of how to bring the tribes usefully into the economy without destroying their traditions and identity is unanswered. However, there is optimism here, too. Ross Swimmer thinks the future looks bright.

"I have worked for the past nine years and seen tremendous change come about in eastern Oklahoma as a result of the tribe's effort. If we can come anywhere close to duplicating what's been done in the next ten years, I think the change in Oklahoma, and especially eastern Oklahoma, will be marked. I think it will amaze a lot of people."

Maybe. But anyone who knows Oklahoma isn't likely to be amazed by anything.

The American Indian Exposition in Anadarko preserves Oklahoma's rich Indian heritage.

Important Historical Events in Oklahoma

1500s The Kiowa, Commanche, and Kiowa-Apache live and hunt in Oklahoma. The Wichita and Caddo are farmers here.

1541 Coronado reaches Oklahoma while looking for the Seven Cities of Cibola. De Sota follows.

1682 Oklahoma is part of the Louisiana Territory claimed by France.

1803 The United States buys the Louisiana Territory from France.

1819 Five tribes of Indians are forced to leave the southeastern United States and go to Oklahoma along the Trail of Tears.

1834 Indian Territory is officially established.

1861 The Civil War brings people from Indian Territory in on both sides. The fighting causes great destruction and loss of life.

1866 Large parts of Indian Territory are taken away from the five Indian nations as punishment for Confederate sympathies.

1870s Cattle drives begin through Indian lands.

1889 Most of the Indian Territory is occupied by Indians who have been forced to leave other parts of the country. The unassigned lands are opened to white settlement in a land run.

1890 Oklahoma Territory is officially established—an island of white settlement in the middle of the Indian Territory.

1891 The U.S. government begins dissolving the Indian nations by dividing tribal lands. Land runs for white homesteaders continue.

1905 The five tribes call a constitutional convention, inviting white settlers. The convention adopts a constitution for the state of Sequoyah. Congress rejects statehood.

1907 The Twin Territories enter the Union as the state of Oklahoma.

1907 The state capital moves from Guthrie to Oklahoma City.

1930 "Alfalfa Bill" Murray shuts down 3,000 oil wells to control oil prices.

1930s The Great Depression combines with the Dust Bowl to cause terrible hardship in Oklahoma and surrounding states.

1943 Robert S. Kerr becomes the first governor of Oklahoma who was born in the state.

1960s-1970s Several dams are completed, improving Oklahoma's water and power supplies.

Oklahoma Almanac

Nickname. The Sooner State.

Capital. Oklahoma City.

State Bird. Scissortailed flycatcher.

State Flower. Mistletoe.

State Tree. Redbud.

State Motto. *Labor Omnia Vincit* (Labor Conquers All).

State Abbreviations. Okla. (traditional); OK (postal).

Statehood. November 16, 1907, the 46th state.

Government. Congress: U.S. senators, 2; U.S. representatives, 6. **State Legislature:** senators, 48; representatives, 101. **Counties:** 77.

Area. 69,919 sq. mi. (181,089 sq. km.), 18th in size among the states.

Greatest Distances. north/south, 230 mi. (370 km.); east/west/464 mi. (747 km.).

Elevation. Highest: Black Mesa, 4,973 ft. (1,516 m). **Lowest:** 287 ft. (87 m), along the Little River.

Population. 1980 Census: 3,025,266 (18% increase over 1970), 26th in size among the states. **Density:** 43 persons per sq. mi. (17 persons per sq. km.). **Distribution:** 67% urban, 33% rural. **1970 Census:** 2,559,463.

Economy. Agriculture: wheat, cotton, peanuts, soybeans, sorghum grain, barley, oats, beef cattle. **Manufacturing:** nonelectrical machinery, oil field machinery; petroleum and coal products, fabricated metal products. **Mining:** petroleum, natural gas, coal, crushed stone, sand and gravel.

Places to Visit

Creek Capital in Okmulgee.
Fort Sill, near Lawton.
National Cowboy Hall of Fame and Western Heritage Center in Oklahoma City.
Tsa-La-Gi Indian Village, near Tahlequah.
Washita Battlefield, near Cheyenne.
Will Rogers Memorial in Claremore.
Woolaroc Museum, near Bartlesville.

Annual Events

Cimarron Territory Celebration in Beaver (April)
Pioneer Days in Guymon (May).
World Championship Watermelon Seed Spittin' Contest in Paul's Valley (June).
American Indian Exposition in Anadarko (August).
Bluegrass Music Festival in Hugo (August).
State Fair of Oklahoma in Oklahoma City (September).

Oklahoma Counties

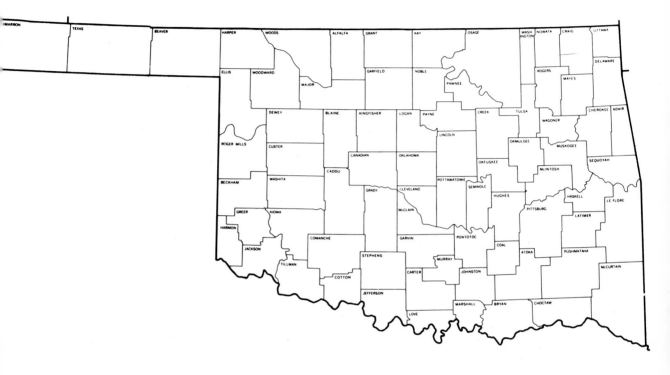

INDEX